THOROUGHFARES

TO LOVE

Diana Shellenberger

Odonata Press   Colorado

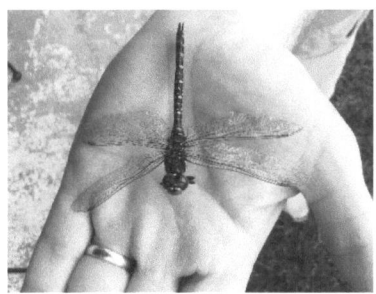

THOROUGHFARES

TO LOVE

Diana Shellenberger

Thoroughfares to Love
© 2017 Diana Shellenberger

ISBN-13: 978-0692868874

Cover and interior photos and interior design by Diana Shellenberger.

All rights reserved. No part of this publication may be reproduced by any means existing or to be developed in the future without written consent from the publisher.

Published in the United States by:

Odonata Press
P.O. Box 714
Longmont, Colorado 80502
www.odonatapress.com

Acknowledgments

Thanks to all careful and caring readers, especially Eric Nickell, Morey Bean, Susan Ross, Sophie Van Tiggelen, Bonney Forbes, Bill Forbes, Marie Perea and Donna Daniell. And especially to Don Murray, my husband and greatest benefactor.

Special thanks to my friend and photographer extraordinaire, Lucy Tuck of Lucy Tuck Photography, for taking my author photograph.

Table of Contents

5	Acknowledgments
8	Poetic Meditation
13	To the Bone
16	Crow-Magnon Woman
19	Of Motorcycles, Life and Love
20	My Road
21	Tributaries
22	Birth
23	Suspense
24	Spiritual Plumber
25	Waterfall
26	Compassion
28	Grace
30	Perpetual Frontier
33	Generator
34	The Wisdom of Stillness
36	Thoroughfares to Love
37	A Sailor's Tale
39	Late Harvest
42	Still Life
45	Perennial Questions
47	Buffalo Grass
50	Power to Love
51	The Language of Nature
53	Plain Speech
58	Dance Steps
61	Everything Comes out in the Wash
62	Local Honey
64	Perfectly Flawed
65	Solid Ground
66	Deep Travel Plan

Poetic Meditation

Love is an infinite topic. Each heart is uniquely structured. Individual are the ways hearts give love, receive love, experience love, make sense of love.

Love can happen instantaneously. The deepest chasm often organizes itself between those who love each other most. They fight each other and the suddenness of their passion, as well as any intimation of loss. Maintaining all loves, whether organic or mystic and ordained, requires a balance between labor and stillness. Grace cannot enter through a swinging door, while trying too hard to preserve love can deliver it stillborn. Holding yourself in reserve has the same result.

One of the poet David Whyte's favorite themes is sincerity. If walking away from love is easy, then did you really mean it? Was it a love of convenience and leisure, a feather bed of love, that you leap up from as soon as you roll onto something uncomfortable? Hitting the hard places is when lovers make progress as couples and individuals. You've merely cleared away the overgrowth and are now entering into the internal structure of what you're creating together.

Resilience is love's friend. Love can last beyond a lifetime if it, and the people who love, keep evolving. It dies a slow, painful death when a few mid-season fruits taste bitter, or when the lovers seek to re-enact the passion that first blossomed between them. Because what once was never re-materializes, they declare love dead and gone. Best to keep eating. Better-tasting fruit depends on it.

Love's life cycle is incomplete without its dissolution. Even as love ends through divorce or death, it has a half life. The shared connection has been severed. But like an amputated limb it is connected to the pathways love creates within and between lovers, and it experiences phantom feelings of every kind.

Love is not only sweet. It has all the danger endemic to adventure. Love is a series of roads, one leading to the next, bridging the past to the future. You do not know where it's going, and you never will.

All roads lead to love. Not just the juiciest, most delicious love of all, romantic love, but domestic love, agape love, and the highest-wire love of all, self-love. This last has so many twists and turns, breakdowns and dead ends, small wonder so few achieve it. Many take the self-pity or self-aggrandizement exits, without ever bothering to return to the main artery.

Love is life's blood. The two are intertwined. Love well, and chances are good you will live well.

Love awakens the eternal within you beyond words and reason and action and time. In this book of poems, I describe it anyway.

Diana Shellenberger
Colorado

THOROUGHFARES TO LOVE

Diana Shellenberger

To the Bone

I was bred in the fight and
raised by some of the best
warriors. Resistance came as
naturally as blood flow and breath

Anger my first response,
the most powerful emotion
no one can ignore
I grew up believing
anger fueled all feeling

Ours is a warring race
but as I grew I learned
others can love more gently
making fewer demands
Given my early training
I mistook it for tepidity
No one was going to tell me
to cool down

I confused love and war
When I felt my love slinking away
I gathered reinforcements
and took aim at him
whose back I perceived was
turned against me

when as a non-combatant
he was merely fleeing
my unfriendly fire

In the world I'd created
hatred's ferocity trumped
love's pliancy
Every
Time.

He was supposed to love me
or else
He was supposed to love me
in the ways I needed to be loved
though he never offered such gifts
when we first fell in love

Love is an X-ray
You see what's broken
and you fix it
Isn't that how everyone loves?
Don't I mend your broken places
before you even ask?
Why don't you see mine?
Don't you know what to do?

I first noticed your eyes
inquisitive, friendly, enjoying,
blaring I adore you

The words rarely make it to your lips
Your kisses are supposed to speak for themselves
This is not a code I can read
I demand to hear the words
I am not assured of your love without them

***

No one comes to love prepared and complete
with an outline plotting the
execution of your loving
It is not a test of your ability to love
or your loveability
but a test of your capacity to raise
your infantile love to adulthood

Love isn't a right
or a prize to be won
We learn to love as we go
as we learn practically everything else—
playing, listening, falling, forgiving

A doctor advises me to take
calcium supplements as more than
fifty years of living on a planet
that eventually reclaims
all the minerals it lent
is exacting payment

In my secret heart I know
my bones are breaking
because of the way I love

It is the privilege of loving you to the bone

Crow-Magnon Woman

Every morning I wake earlier than the rest
like a kid at Christmas eager to see what
Santa Crow brings today
I am quiet for as long as I can be
No sotto voce here
a hoarse reveille at top volume
on key and on time

I light on a fence
joined by my best friends for now
we test our balance
on the narrow split rails
a murder of crows we're called
(we think of ourselves as a cawfee klatsch)

We're well aware we're bad ass
in our shiny black feather jackets
beaks the circumference of cigarillos
We're also aware you call us scavengers
Very well.
But excuse me we
never
murder
anything
We clean with style
the messes others leaves behind

To break my fast
I feast on a squirrel's remains
fresh-killed in morning traffic

I time my flights with the approach of cars
waiting til the last second to
nonchalantly float to a light post before

I resume picking at my
Squirrel Atop Blacktop
playing to the spontaneous rhythm
of flight-disruption-return
syncopated like jazz
with movement and
the slow flapping of wings as accompaniment

My bark is worse than my peck but
attack my nest its belly
full of babies and I bear down
with the intensity of a locomotive
eyes on high beam behind
a beak of iron
opening the soft places
of your body

Lest you dismiss me as nothing more
than a housecrow
I see all manner of comings and goings
from my suburban perches, where humans
behave as if they were here first—
Forgive them.
They know not what bad neighbors they are.

Though they don't mean it so—
God's love conquers every stinginess
and every excess—
people love more than they know
through the mayhem their cars cause
and the leavings they consider trash

A human made pattern of days
overlays the accidental, the wild, the purposeless
I don't so much live my life
as life lives on through me

Chaos preys on the order imposed
by those who cannot accept
there is no order
only a play where no one knows their lines

Of Motorcycles, Life and Love

My mom was seventeen when her uncle
taught her how to ride his motorcycle
to balance, steer and accelerate

She was having the ride of her life—
until she wanted to stop.
That's when she realized
the lesson was incomplete
She aimed the machine
for a barbed wire fence
which stopped her, all right.
To this day she bears the scar on her forearm

This is the way I love
I know how to start
how to accelerate
But God help me
I have no idea
how to stop

My Road

At the four corners we say our goodbyes
As you walk away
I watch your fragile spine
A sob sticks in my throat
as the pain you live with
combines with mine

I consider catching up with you
and begging
to let me accompany you

But I know the road you've chosen
is not my road, even if I was welcome to take it

Mine continues straightaway
I see the far-off peaks we once vowed
to climb together
My feet small and light
on the road's broad back

We arrive separately at our next destinations
I'm grateful
you helped get me as far as I am today

Tributaries

One tributary in the river of my life
has dried up, its bed the skeleton
of my child-bearing years
Like life itself I knew
these days could never last
but secretly believed they would

Yet the habit of expectancy persists

Though the energy of this stream
has ceased without the monthly
blood draw and the tending of my
childrens' burgeoning lives
some latent vitality
may yet present itself
A trickle I once considered a rogue leak
could well develop into a new stream

My womanhood isn't ending
Like the moon that governs
all manner of tides
it's entering a new phase

Birth

Every month my nest would feather itself
preparing for an egg to nestle within
and become new life

Now the monthly blood has stopped.

And yet
I enter into a period no less fecund
I'm free to leave the nest
to give birth to aspects of myself
that develop more slowly
than my sons did in utero

Their bodies formed within mine
as miracles do—following a recipe not mine
sequentially and silently

Midlife birth requires a longer gestation
one I more consciously abet
still subject to mystery
awaiting miracles
and also with something to give:
a yolk of what I once was
to feed what I am becoming

Suspense

I dream my family is on a road trip
The road ends abruptly, and the car
leaps in mid-air toward the roof of a
tall building. With our sons in the car,
my husband steers best he can

The car lands on the roof but
the driver's side wheels are over the edge
Again he steers away from catastrophe
but momentum is not in our favor
The car is heading off the roof.
I think, This is it. This is how it ends.

Before, when I imagined a fatal crash,
I predict I would waste valuable oxygen panicking
In my dream I stay calm considering
we are all about to lose everything.

My husband's cancer treatment is the leap
from road's end to rooftop
We're in mid-air now.
Time will tell how we land.

Faith in his power to heal
modern medicine
and God
keeps us aloft in the buoyant suspension
we've always been in and
couldn't appreciate until now

Spiritual Plumber

I wake to the sound of water running

My in-house plumber away for the night
I rise to inspect every faucet and toilet
and discover an irrigation system valve is leaking

I turn it off and go back to bed
to think about other plumbing problems
disturbing my sleep

Adults have a terrible power
to sheathe a child's wildness in politeness
accidentally closing off
valves of creativity and confidence
while the ones that water weeds
flow freely

Finding and stopping
a leak's source
is only one step
toward allowing
the streams within
to nourish seeds that feed

Waterfall

I hear the waterfall before I see it
relentlessly pounding bedrock into grains of sand
I feel its power beneath my feet and inside my chest
like music slipping inside a crevice revealing itself

I am not in the waterfall's midst only close
enough to feel droplets and know its coolness
I am not sufficiently fearless—
fearlessness precedes courage—
to withstand its torrents of heavy fast water
ladling itself atop my head

My spine might be crushed
not to mention my will
I have long been the toddler declaring
"I do it myself!"
Like an indulgent parent, God allows it

I see now the illusion:
My hands a blur of activity
rarely and accidentally serving Purpose while

God's Hands are invisibly active
with one finger brushing aside a curtain
moving boulders obstructing my path
showing me the way

Compassion

In a dream I watch a bearded young man
operating a pogo stick on a grassy hillside

Is that a good idea? I wonder
Apparently so, as he makes one improbable
hop after another, slaloming with feet of virtuosity

until he loses his balance and tumbles downhill

His fall stops a long way from where it began
but even from a distance I can see blood
streaming from his nose and mouth

We need to call 9-1-1, I say to my companion
as I watch the injured man crawl onto a bench
his arms draping over the back
his legs splayed

Every day people take terrible falls
and no one comes to their aid

Thinking about helping is not the same as helping
The young man can rightly believe
I am bleeding and no one is coming

I don't know what to do.
I don't know if I can handle seeing so much blood
if I even want to be so close to blood
his body no longer contains

He was playing, and play can go as horribly wrong
as an argument can take a sudden turn for the worse
becoming a bruising and even bloody battle

Who are these people who appear during disasters
who seem to know just what to do
In the moment Grace infuses them

Untapped goodness rests within everyone
Most save it up until the world is a war zone

And even then most of us stand
safely at the top of the hill
watching as other human beings bleed

I wish I had run down the hill to be with him
allowing myself to see what cannot be unseen
to comfort what cannot be comforted

Because wouldn't I want someone
anyone
to be with me when I'm hurting?

Grace

A crow practices the
art of surrender in
a windstorm, crumpling like
a piece of shiny black
paper, played and playing

In dreams I outwit captors
and escape, knowing when,
where and for how long
to hide. Waking I hope
for more than survival

Leaving Grandpa's ranch on a
Montana blue-sky day, three
sisters cry. Journey's rhythm,
like mother's arms, lulls them
into trading sobs for sleep

The Navajo call
January babies
Eagle People, beaks
breaking through frozen eggshells.
Winter hatched toughness

He and I severed the threads
connecting us one by
one. We fell to the ground,
arguing over who
made the final cut

Life is a tightrope
stretching between birth and
death. Suspended, only sometimes
sure of foot, best to balance
moving inward and forward

A shearwater plunges from
cloudy sky to restless sea,
in time with a whale's grace-full
leap delivering fish from
the depths to the surface

All is a dance, subject to
timing, partnership, desire,
endurance, gravity, practice,
enjoyment,
given to each
in different measure

Perpetual Frontier

The road stretches
like a sun-blackened pelt
through the desert

Travelers seek
a perpetual frontier
delivering
connection
   new beginnings
      eternity

and an emptiness so great
their own dissolves into it
like a stray raindrop
on the arid land

I am driving far and fast
away from a love
that ended too soon

The road is in the same condition
as my spirit
scarred
lined and pocked
Yet both are still passable

I hit the gas
to speed over rises
that lift my gut into my heart,
the lightest it's been in days

The long drive allows me
to practice being alone
in the comfortable discomfort
of deserted places

The strangers I meet
who run the gas stations
and motels from the last century
for whom hardship
is daily bread
don't know what I've lost
and why

At twilight
I pull into a campground
pitch my tent
open a beer
lay down on the ground
to look up at the stars
sparkling like straight pins
in a black velvet pincushion

I'm in a time and a place
wild humans once traversed
They were people
who saw gods in the stars

The daylong lights of the city
bleach the constellations
severing people
from our forebears'
instinct and imagination

As my eyes adjust to
the night's balanced formula
of darkness and starlight
I could swear
the vastness of the sky
stoops to draw near
as the ground cradles me

In such a pitiless place
there is no time for self-pity
only self-reflection
in the clean mirrors
of land and sky

Generator

"I prayed for love and realized it's always knocking, but I have to allow it in."—Rumi

When the snow falls deep
or the winds blow strong
a friend who lives in the mountains
loses power to her home
Then a generator keeps
her furnace, lights and appliances working

As Earth's winter axis shifts away from the sun
our love turns cold
and a succession of storms
cuts the lines between our hearts

I set out to search for a generator to make me go and glow
I walk through the snow in the darkness
seeking the warmth of belonging somewhere, to someone

Even as I explore my inner realm
making my way each day with each step
toward my own God-given
eternal internal pilot light
still I want to warm myself
beside someone else's fire

The Wisdom of Stillness

When the ground beneath my feet
got too hot, I used to run
seeking cooler ground

Everywhere I ran the heat was on
I slowly discovered
what was raising the temperature:
the friction
of my feet striking the ground

Friends counseled me to sit.
Rest. Take a load off.
Pace myself.

Staying in one place
was a prescription I didn't need
when what I wanted
was to experience more, to be more
I kept running until my soles burned
until sitting was my only option

The more I sat the more I understood
the heat's true source—
I had mastered the manufacture of struggle
My living generated the fire

My study and practice of the wisdom of stillness
teaches me to collect concentration
like raindrops in a well
Before long the ground and my feet cooled

Peace is not subject to command
It does not respond to raised voices
and snapping fingers

It comes after a sustained period
of bucking, hissing and pinging
like an overheating engine
long after the ignition is shut off

Stillness welcomes me
Becoming its guest
and its host
takes a lifetime

I have discovered my true strength
lies not in how much ground I cover
but how connected to the ground I am

Thoroughfares to Love

How do you come to love life
in all its blight and blessing?

Do you know what life costs?
Is there a fare structure that allows
you to keep tabs, adding good times
and multiplying bad, dividing
storms and subtracting thimbles full of rain?

There are moments when you thoroughly love
your life and your ability to love is effortless,
other times when you despair
because you have no memory
of when you were ever truly loved
in all the beatified brokenness
you yourself never appreciate

Just as you believed you never saved anything or anyone
but were yourself a burden upon the Earth
somehow life and love accrue to your benefit

A road opens up its turnstile spinning freely
admitting you to a passage long ago written
by and for you

A Sailor's Tale

The way dolphins swim together
diving and resurfacing
their snouts breaching the waves
at different intervals
is a reminder
of how couples
fall in and out of love

An old sailor observed
in sailing as in living
we're mostly drifting off course

He fought wind and wave—
denying each moment's potency
mad at the elements thwarting his plans
and hating his puniness—
to return to a time and place
long ago melted into memory.

I wanted smooth sailing, he said,
and got wisdom instead.

We hate Life for staying wild.
Like Pharisees we attempt
to codify what is of the Spirit
and beyond any law

Forgive Life

We fight over what we've already
gained and lost
a million times over
playing keep away with
the best times we've shared

Forgive each other

For a thousand dawns
I watched you as you slept
and found you as perfect
as the babies we made together
But with every cross word
Or missed handoff
I forget

Forgive me

Because I am a slow learner
and because I want
as much time with you
as I can get
I pray for a long life

Late Harvest

Why do some people fulfill life's promise
faster than others?
I look to berry bushes for answers
and discover more questions

Why does fruit on the same stalk
ripen at different times?
Each berry is exposed to sunlight and moisture

Is there a shadow I cannot see
blocking blessing from some
as others absorb the full impact?

Life isn't fair.

From where I stand
we are either bending toward justice
or justifying our privilege

Like fruit ripening life is
not always ready to eat
when we're hungriest

In the meantime
we eat only what nourishes
but does not satisfy
what keeps us living
rather than alive.

We don't see we are getting fat
for a late harvest

I have long vied for the early summer harvest
forgetting that some of the best produce
arrives late in the season

I have impatiently awaited my harvest
forgetting that those fruits first to ripen
are also first to be eaten
abetting another's growth

Mine has been happening all along
I have held and nurtured life
growing strong and tall
for others' enjoyment and sustenance

Like most things
I grow without noticing
So much reveals itself
in the fullness of time

I have taken longer to emerge
It would seem I have been
green and sour beyond my season

I believed I had to benefit,
to grow rich and renowned,
fruit juice dripping down my chin

When true power lies
in repeating season upon season
Life's Cycle:
Leaf, Blossom, Fruit and Harvest
as many times as I am privileged

Still Life

de Zurbaran's painting
of lemons on a gilt plate
oranges and blossoms in a basket
a cup of coffee adorned with a rose
lined up on a dust-free table
is all so fresh and perfect
knowing it can't last
almost breaks my heart

The cat jumps on the table
pollen grains blow in through an open window
a phone rings
the rose sheds a petal
the orange blossoms lose fragrance
to the air itself
changing direction

Proving life is not still
and cannot be stilled
though the artist tries
to capture moments
without lament
with joy

The tang of the citrus
the sweetness of blossoms
coffee's eternal perfume
is perfectly familiar
One element is missing—
I expect to see a trace of steam above the coffee

Until I consider
that maybe Señor Z
likes his coffee cooled.
Within the frame
he decides.

The movement of life is like
the orbit of a star tracing a trail
no other can follow
its progression
There is beauty even in its death.

From where I stand a star appears
to shoot across the sky
before extinguishment.
A scar remains where
the star once shone.

I am preoccupied with stars and scars.
Life excludes neither
and nothing.
Life is an invitation to follow.

Not that I can keep up.
I can only keep it within memory's sight
the perfection of the arrangement
of each moment
the flowers the fruit the coffee
the star alive, shooting, and extinguished
enjoyed on terms not mine

The artist does not so much attempt
to control nature but to reflect it.

Kilmer says a poem
can never be lovelier
than a tree

People make things because
our Creator makes things
and we are made
in Her image.

The artist brings things to life
as life brings things to her
arranging them
and yes, even
ordering them like
tiles in a mosaic
points of color and light in a portrait
events in a life

What makes most sense in the moment
is not always chronological
and why there's such a thing as infinity

The best I hope to do
with the game of Scrabble
I call poetry
is to represent the recombinant
kaleidoscopic
patterns of life

Using a palette of feeling
recollection
movement
knowledge
imposes its own order
independent of my desire
to express myself

An artist does not still life
Only a hunter can
She brings life to art
and art to life

Perennial Questions

How much do you love me?
my mom and I would ask
flinging our arms open as wide
as our hearts could stretch

I have since played variations
of the game with lovers

Reporting some loves have
expiration dates gives me no cheer
They perish from
deficiency
excess
imbalance
timing
Under these conditions
the odds are against
love taking root

Hearts of love want to grow
but how much? And for how long?
the perennial questions

I tend many gardens
My taste runs toward the tangled and thorny
rife with fruit ripening at different tempos

You prefer your garden
to grow slow and mannerly

Bonsai offers the marvel
of concentrating Nature

My patience runs along other lines
A tree grows tall and wide only
after years of tending and waiting
for shade, shelter and fruit

Your love is no less sincere than mine

I enjoy different
expressions of desire
and hope we visit each
other's gardens often

I don't want to force you to grow
any faster than you wish

I also hope you'll understand
I could never bonsai
when I have the chance
to grow an enormous tree

Buffalo Grass

On Colorado's high plains
the bison were here first
along with the grass they fed on

The herds are long since decimated
but the grasses remain
spreading in dense mats

No medicine is strong enough
to eradicate them
Their persistence proves
Providence's bell is not
easily unrung

Montana ranching relatives
call it quackgrass
others still, crabgrass
I call it buffalo grass
a name worthy of respect
that properly suggests its strength

Every few weeks in summer
I do my own battle with buffalo grass
on a south facing gravel path
with weapons no more lethal
than a spade and my bare hands

Dig six inches and I succeed
in pulling up the grassy growth
and only some of the root
long and thin as a baby asparagus stalk
and tough as cable

Occasionally I pull up a clump of roots
which is satisfying
until I realize I've torn away
only a bit of the wily underlying roots
that grow sideways and connect
cat's-cradle style
knowing as all living systems do
the strength in numbers
and connection

Together they reach to
the center of the earth
dispatching more shoots
for my digging displeasure

In spiritual practice
Only occasionally do you
unearth the root systems
of past action and dilemma
to the same effect as buffalo grass

Yet the very act of digging
makes you stronger and
motivates you to continue working

All is on a trajectory of growth,
of being true to its nature
grass and weeds
the human animal

The Creator does not prefer one
above the other
because She sees all as good,
even very good

The Sun is God's face
beaming at all equally
the buffalo grass and me

Power to Love

At the beginning I thought you were perfect
I thought I might be perfect too
because we had finally met

The difference between
love and war is the same
as the difference
between polishing and scouring

Most of us choose abrasion
eroding and adding blemishes
when we could be refining
and adding luster

I hold you up to the light
and can't tell the difference
until you say something that feels
unkind or untrue or reminds me
of my belief that no one
who knows me could ever
truly love me

Then I blame you
for casting a shadow
when the black cloud
obscuring my power to love
hung long before we met

I've failed to love myself
through many storms, exposing myself
to the battery of hail
and the lashing of rain

But you inspire me to build
a hospitable little shelter to share with you

The Language of Nature

A yogini worthy of the name
teaches you how to listen
with the ears of the heart

I have a teacher
so advanced in her practice
such a good student of listening
along the way she also learned
to speak from her heart
a place so deep, sweet and whole
a purewater well
I lean in to hear
her voice amid the echoes

Meanwhile I fuss over my words
to say what I want
the best way I know how
as if words are the letter of the law
rather than a reflection of spirit

I seek friends who speak
the same language
or are at least willing to learn
as I am willing to be multilingual
to hear and to speak
as children do
making understanding as they stumble

We all of us want to be understood,
even those who hear St. Francis of Assisi's advice
Seek not so much to be understood as to understand
but cannot yet heed it

Listening returns us to hearing,
our most durable sense

Carbon monoxide poisoned my grandmother
a nest in the chimney trapped the gas inside the house
She heard the fireman say, *She's gone*
She felt herself screaming *No, I'm here! I'm alive!*

She couldn't see.
She couldn't move.
She couldn't make herself heard.
She could hear.

Not sure what revived her—
the fireman's premature declaration of her demise
or the power of the voice inside her.

The language of nature is obvious
birdsong, river stories , tree sagas, ocean epics
What interests me is the language
inside the chirps, beneath the water's surface
within the pith of the bristlecone pine
the abiding, instructive tales
patiently waiting within all things
to share with willing hearts
the distillation of centuries of
all they have witnessed
and tasted
and borne

Plain Speech

When I was a little girl my parents wanted me to be good
I didn't like the scolding and paddling I got when I was bad
I tried obedience but saw little reward
I got more attention when I misbehaved

Mostly I wanted to be seen and heard
and to get my way at least occasionally

I loved my grandpa so much
He taught chemistry and physics
hard sciences with indisputable facts

As I grew I was surprised
to find myself disagreeing with him
because I had learned things
in conflict with what he knew

I read the same magazines
the ones he kept on the end table
beside his recliner
We came to very different conclusions
about Vietnam

What did a little girl know about war
and those who would protest it?

I was confused
In catechism I learned killing was a sin

I overheard my grandpa and my parents agree
"Those kids at Kent State had it coming to them"

Kids like me? I wondered
if being shot by police
was like being spanked by your parents

Every spanking I lost a little bit more of their love
as they lost a little bit more of mine

Disagreement can be dangerous.

At school I noticed some of the boys,
the ones I liked—the handsome, intelligent
and strong—disapproved of my challenges
to what they knew was true,
which was and is what I try to get to—the truth

For some being right is an improvement on the truth
The truth is for sissies who can't make up their own minds
about how the world works

I have always been a good and willing student
Eventually the lessons did their magic
I wanted to be good, now
and forever
avoiding the things that got me into trouble—
talking plainly
talking out of turn
talking, talking, talking

Talking in general was evidently
a problem area for me
or so I was told by people
for whom talking was no problem

I wanted to believe advice
that I'd be happier
keeping my "opinions" to myself

I pretended that what I thought
and what I wanted was of less value
than what others thought and wanted

I made my life about serving others
to realize their dreams and offer comfort
when they didn't

Thirty years I walked around with a lump in my throat
a stone in the cave's mouth

But lately a voice
that sounds like mine
but is potent and undeniable
has begun speaking out loud
creating its own language
with its own rules
a voice that feels and sounds true
making sense of all that's happened
and happening
and arranging into a world
I think I could live in

I do not intend to displease
I love harmony when it is true harmony
I failed to thrive under a regime that insists
Peace is the absence of war

I am becoming the kind of religious person
who picks and chooses what I like
what feels true to me
and leaves the rest

What's wrong with not swallowing
every pill I'm offered?
Maybe it's the right medicine for others,
but it makes me sick

I know this
makes me a heretic, a libertine
I might go to hell

Maybe so, if I believed in hell
I'm taking my chances

Being true to myself and deciding what I need
makes this life, here and now, better for me
This is the work of an adult.
I hurt no one.

We live in a world of people who love
every kind of convenience, including
the convenience of a plain-spoken woman's silence
a woman who won't tell you what she wants
but leaves it up to you because
after all she doesn't mind and you're better
at deciding anyway

Fuck that.

I have as much right as anyone to ask for
what I want, without fearing a no
or a yes
What if I actually got to do what I've dreamed of doing?
To become who I've dreamed of becoming?
Would I relish the freedom, the delight, of getting
my heart's desire?

Or would I give it away
to someone who needed it more?
Setting aside my wishes was practically a reflex
Tongue bound for so long, I lost
the connection between my desires
and speaking up for them

Late in life I am learning
to follow the lines of my desires
All of them
Even the ones that get me into trouble with
Speech Enforcement

It's not that I've earned the right
It's that I've had it all along

Dance Steps

The first time I saw Wandile Kabane
I thought he might be Bob Marley
with a South African accent
without dreads
café au lait complexion
delicate features
sensitive eyes
slow wide smile
impossibly slender

We met at a party
hosted by South Africans
When my date and I arrived
people were dancing
to Masekela, Makeba and Madonna
in the host's tiny living room

Someone silenced the music
Everyone formed a circle
and each greeted us with smiles and handshakes

I'd never felt so welcomed
at American parties where
everyone competes
for time with the right people
and alcohol

After the introductions
the music started
People were not so much dancing
as bumping into each other
Wandile asked me to dance
How could I dance with him
when I couldn't even pronounce his name

like dance steps in my mouth
I kept stumbling over
Wan-dee-lay Kah-bah-nay

He told me I moved sensually
right before he kissed me
and not just a chaste gentlemanly peck
but a full-bloom, full-moon howling kiss
right in front of our dates

After that night I saw him
at other parties
I was with the same date
who had forgiven
but not forgotten

During a visit Wandile told me
In my country I would not be allowed
to be with a white girl like you

I told him it wasn't long ago
in certain parts of my country
you would not be allowed
to be with a white girl like me
In fact it was frequently lethal

I got word that Wandile was in jail
A boy at Berkeley called him
a name guaranteed to start a fight
Wandile's reply was to thrust
a broken beer bottle
in the boy's face

Wandile and his countrymen
were homesick
Though apartheid had mistreated them
like a mother South Africa

was the only home
they'd ever known
and wanted to know

I dream he made it home
receiving the same welcome
he and his friends offered me
in the center of a big circle
smiling and shaking hands
dancing with and kissing
whoever he damn well pleases

Everything Comes out in the Wash

"And now faith, hope and love abide, these three; and the greatest of these is love."—1 Corinthians 13:13

That stubborn stain that never comes out
in wash after wash
until the thousandth when it disappeared

I thought it must be a mistake

A laundry gremlin exchanged the garment
for a duplicate, fooling me into believing
my efforts had finally succeeded

That could be true, believing as I do in magic

More likely the steady march
of hope, faith and especially love
through the battlefields of my life
faded the stain

Local Honey

What if I had known all along
that not knowing what
to do with my life
was exactly right for me?

For thirty-odd years I thought
something was missing
or I was missing something—
which I was, though not what I thought

I was like a honeybee
who had lost her bearings
I had a taste for something
I couldn't navigate my way to

So few of the flowers I landed on
had the flavor I sought
and the sustenance I craved

I traveled on in search of both
relying on others' good opinions of me
Those too were scarce
The road is full of people in need
with little left to give or lose

A few arrows pointed in my direction
I saw and didn't believe
there was anything to go to

except a ghost town
where some hopefuls had once
built homes
made a modest living
raised a couple of generations

until

a flood a tornado a fire a landslide
felled hope like trees
Without fruit or shade
I abandoned myself

until

A vein of sweetness
flowing sun-flavored honey
emptied itself
into the dry hollow
where my heart beat blandly

Local honey is the best
pure and wholesome
It contains the nectar
of millions of flowers
the spit, sweat, toil and
yes, love
of free-living bees

Thirty years of foraging
the fields of my life
believing I had lost my way
when I had been instead
perfecting the art of wandering
collecting the nectar
converting itself
to treasure all along

Perfectly Flawed

Most of the serving platters I own are chipped
hand-me-downs from Depression-era grandmas
I've put the few I've split in two
back into service with super glue
They hold food just as well as before their fall

What if the chink in your armor
you've tried to hide, guard or fill
is a portal to your perfection?
That the flaw is not a weakness
but the source of your greatest strength?

You fall, break, and put yourself back together
many times in your life's Integrity Play relearning
vulnerability is a better teacher than impenetrability

Solid Ground

A girl my age, fourteen at the time,
was for days trapped beneath rubble
an earthquake wrought

Her rescuers lifted her, thin and limp
from what might have been her tomb
and instead served as a kind of womb,
the building's broken shell protecting
if not nourishing her

People take breathing for granted
Disaster makes everything scarce

During the hours of her second enwombment
she learned to be thrifty with her breath
counting each as she had once counted the stars
above the Italian village where she was born

Others near her had not been so lucky
The building that had seemed so solid before the quake
with rhythmic chaos crushed life

I want to believe her life took a permanently mystic turn
recalling forever the grace that had spared her
devoting herself to saving other souls
despite proof most of us can barely save our own

We have all survived ordeals
and risen to live out our days
forgetting to count our blessings of breath and stars
as we seek solid ground beneath our feet

Deep Travel Plan

"It's always ourselves we love the least
That's the burden of the angel beast"
—Bruce Cockburn

Experts say it's best
for infants to crawl
before they walk
to best ensure
orderly overall development

Maybe this is why
our race struggles
People continually buck sequence
rearranging the map
to suit themselves
succeeding only
in getting lost

When my sons were babies
I was most concerned
in this order
about being a good mother
tending their growth and comfort
and wanting them to learn
what they need to know
to have successful lives

I am late in realizing
the real work of parenting
is teaching children
to love their lives,
and themselves

Life is more than
a journey on an interstate
straight shots
clearly marked entrance exams
and exit interviews
evenly spaced
rest stops with clean toilets
and truck stops that serve
predictably mediocre food

Expect to turn off
at undesignated exit ramps
following frontage roads
to gravel arteries
leading to distant bridges
and farmhouses
when you are waylaid
with engine trouble

Hours seemingly go by
without the approach of another car
until a mid-twentieth century pickup
appears, and two quiet men inspect
your broken down late-model vehicle
scratching their heads before offering
you a tow for repairs
in the nearest big town
forty miles away

In the meantime
they take you to one of the farmhouses
you passed fifteen miles ago
where women who barely
speak your language
welcome you into a clean kitchen
smelling of breakfast

where they serve you pie
hot out of the oven
and as you eat
they wash your dusty clothes

Life is an adventure
love the lesson
we learn in patterns
that meet us when
we are most, and least, ready

We plan, while the Deep Travel Plan
guides us along roads
visible only in dreams

Can you love your life enough
to trust your goodness
and where your journey leads,
no matter what happens?

Thoroughfares to Love is Diana Shellenberger's first book of poetry. She lives in Colorado with her husband.

www.ingramcontent.com/pod-product-compliance
Lightning Source LLC
Chambersburg PA
CBHW041527090426

42736CB00036B/222